A World without States

Dago Steenis

A WORLD WITHOUT STATES

Aspekt Publishers

A WORLD WITHOUT STATES
© Dago Steenis
© 2016 Uitgeverij ASPEKT / Aspekt Publishers
Amersfoortsestraat 27, 3769 AD Soesterberg, The Netherlands
info@uitgeverijaspekt.nl – http://www.uitgeverijaspekt.nl

Cover: Maarten Bakker
Inside: Thomas Wunderink

ISBN: 9789463380362
NUR: 130

All rights reserved. No reproduction copy or transmission of this publication may be made without written permission.

CONTENTS:

Humanity is Anchored in the evolution of existence   7

Preface   11

I. The Age in which we Live   **15**
The Current Political System   17
The Growth of Humanitarianism   19
Violence is never the Answer   21
Empathy: Us and the Others   25
Existence: From Nature to Culture   28

II. The Emergence of the State   **31**
Communities begin to Organize   33
States sometimes turn into Empires   36
The State Guards its Ownership   37
The State Guards its Identity   40
The State Promotes Nationalism   42
The State Guards its Sovereignty   43
The State Demands Obedience   45
The State Threatens Peace   47
The System of States Leads to Armaments   49
Globalisation   52

III. The Final Crisis of the Transitium   **55**
Chaos and Inhumanity   57
The Bloodbath of the Colonisation of Africa   59
The Bloodbath of the First World War   63
The League of Nations Clings to the System of States   66
The Bloodbath of the Second World War   69
The Uno and the Blood Baths in the Rebellious Colonies   73
The Balance of the Twentieth Century   78

IV: The United States Enforces its Standards on the World   **81**
The American World Order   83
Saddam Hussein's Role   85

THE DESTINATION OF MAN

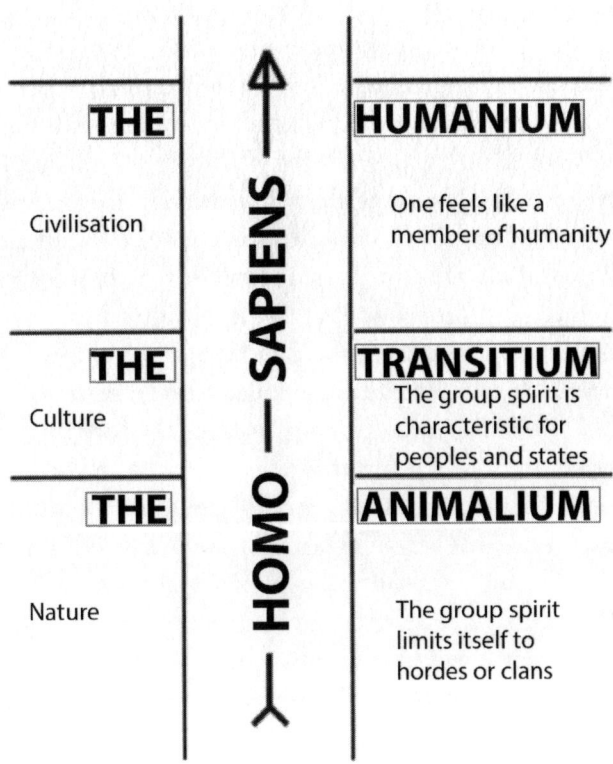

HUMANITY IS ANCHORED IN THE EVOLUTION OF EXISTENCE

Reader, if you calmly look at this diagram you will behold the evolution of human existence. Man began life as an animal. The period of the animalistic existence of man is called The Animalium in the diagram. People lived in small communities, hurdles, and secured their food by means of hunting animals and gathering all the edible things that nature offers.

Evolution shows an ascending line. A time dawns in which the species of man transcends the animal existence through the discovery of culture. That is, the start of agriculture and cattle-breeding, approximately ten thousand years ago. Since then culture has developed more powerfully. Today the term culture represents 'everything that characterizes human society'. The surface of the earth has changed from being nature into culture. It is a time in which man still displays primitive, animal-like behaviour, but on the other hand evolves in the direction of humanity. The age of this mixed culture is called The Transitium.

In today's speech this age is called 'history'. Historians merely focus on this period. Placed in the hundreds of thousands of years of evolution of human existence, this period of ten thousand years is no more than a short transitioning period from animality to humanity. It would be great if people in education and science would realize this and pass it on.

At one glance the diagram shows what man's destination is: the Transitium needs to make way for a time in which humanity will have triumphed in world society. We will experience an age of civilisation. In the diagram this age is called the Humanium, the age of humanity.

However, culture has not yet reached this stage. The residents on earth still reside in the Transitium, in which animality and humanity are still mixed together, an era that does not focus on lasting peace, and permits too little humanity.

Together we need to ensure that we leave the Transitium behind as soon as possible, and that we, as humans, reach our destination.

The destination of man is becoming completely humane.

The Humanium will be a time of lasting peace and mutual respect, a time of equal rights for everyone on earth, of prosperity and equal opportunities for all.

Isn't this some kind of utopia, a dream that will never become a reality?

That is certainly not the case, where there's a will, there's a way.

Let all peace-loving individuals join forces and work together to ensure a better world.

How do we do that?

This book is dedicated to exactly that problem.

Preface

The world is turning at different speeds. Due to the increasing globalization this has become clearer than ever before. The attentive news follower can read encouraging news every day, of rapprochement, bridging, and progressive insights, but also exclaim because of the resilience of human beings and the diligence with which mistakes are repeated. In addition to integration, disintegration, removal, nationalism, wars, and religious fanaticism are unfortunately omnipresent. These processes play out simultaneously.

I say processes because sociology mainly focused, for a large part of the twentieth century, on components or news, which overshadowed the more long-term trends in politics and society. A long-term vision is essential to keep a handle on the contradictions of the misconceptions of the day. The far-reaching politicisation of the twentieth century and the resulting dogmas have left a mark on history. In an attempt to turn loose facts into a transparent whole, a process, some speak of a 'sociogenesis', a structuring of the world is necessary.

Dago Steenis resides in this tradition. For centuries man has been the pawn of emotions, coincidences, volatilities of nature, or of unreliable small particularistic political interests and public authorities. Initially it seemed that the emergence of state and nation brought forward an organization that could ensure stability, peace, and civilisation. However, the Napoleonic era in the nineteenth century, and, above all, the disastrous twentieth century, were a radical spanner in the works. The modern nation state did not guarantee peace, and the monopoly on violence caused by the state was used against neighbouring countries and its own people. In Western Europe the National Socialism was an absolute low point. In Eastern Europe, roughly the area east of the river Elbe, was in the Twentieth century mostly governed by the old imperial riches, the Hapsburg, Ottoman, and Russian empire and its successors, all characterized by a systematic oppression of man and human rights. It is for a reason that the decisive element of Steenis' work is that the world needs to revise the widely accepted presence of the concept of state. Indeed, the world would be better off in a stateless world.

Dago Steenis (1925) has written a remarkably positive book, something that is actually more than a book, it is a thought that can be passed on, a manual even. Not like a pamphlet, but based on his speech, metabletic, the teachings of change. According to Steenis history cannot be a linear concept, nor a static process, without progress. On the contrary. History precisely demonstrates that we have a reason to be optimistic. The developments of mankind are evolutionary, and an increasing form of human growth and potency. As a result Steenis talks about a 'universal evolution', and this culture is 'man-made'.

We are therefore in control and work has to be done. First it concerns the concept of state, something that Steenis feels limits the 'New World Order' that should emerge from the metabletic evolution. With it Steenis, in many respects, adds to the civilising theory of Norbert Elias. After all, Elias advocated that the rise of the modern states ended the days of dark chaos in the antiquity and middle ages. Ever since the lessons taught to us by the twentieth century and the world wars, an annotation has been added, inter alia via sociologist Tonnes Zwaan, that states do not only civilise, but also 'de-civilise', as was the case with Nazi-Germany. Today Steenis transcends that discussion by pointing out the inevitability of the universal evolution that announces itself, that the supporting role of the state will further marginalize, and that the role of man, the 'civil society', is given more leeway.

Some of you might immediately think of a utopia. However, history is filled with pivots and tipping points in which matters of technical nature (the turning plough), or technological nature (electricity, steam, and digital revolution) brought about a new horizon for mankind. The humanities also include many of these turning and tipping points. Wherever these will end up will be determined by history. However, Steenis' book is at least a more than an interesting introduction of a process that is probably already unfolding below the surface. Has he correctly read the signs of times? The fact that today one is dealing with very large almost elusive discontent, also in large parts of the Western world, no one can deny. Elections in Europe and the United States emphasize that the middle ground is losing ground due to a lack of legitimacy. Answers from the past seem to slowly lose their value. The world is looking and becoming more and more rudderless. The degree of doubt about even the most basic political decisions, with the migration issues as the result of the unrest in the Middle East – are a clear example.

Now that courses are changing new frames of thinking are required. Dago Steenis offers us one. His position in the civilisation discussion from Elias to Zwaan, to his own theories is more than interesting. It can give rise to discussion that is true, it is bold, surprising, at times even curious, but sometimes the noise comes from the 'outside'. Heinrich Schliemann dug up Troy, not the professors. Now it is up to the reader to judge this book.

Dr. Perry Pierik.

The Islamic Radicalisation 91
The Arab World in Motion 93

V: Terror and Anti-Terror **97**
'The War on Terror' 99
Civil War and Refugees 102

VI: Counter-Moment: Growth of Humanity **107**
From Chaos to Renewal 109
Pleas for Humanity 113
A Humane Attitude towards Animals 115
The Peace Movement 118
Defense against the Maltreatment of the Planet 120
Rapid Growth of Humanitarian Organisations 122

VII: Evolution and Progress **125**
Evolution as Leading Concept 127
What could a World Government do? 130

I

The Age in which we Live

The Current Political System

Humanity is still living in the Transitium, an age characterized by, among others, wars, violence, and inhumanity. No wonder. Today the entire surface of the earth is divided into states, communities that focus on their own interests. It is the system of states that forms a barrier for the quick and effective approach to major problems, such as lasting peace, security, and the habitability of the earth. After all, these are global problems. The system of states divides humanity into hostile units, and forms a political barrier for a solution of it.

States focus on their own interests. States are on edge when it comes to their sovereignty, their right to maintain individuality without outside interference. They wish to always maintain and protect it. The inhabitants of a state feel like a people, a nation. They expect only one thing from their government: that it properly represents the interests of its own people. Many people quickly become suspicious when the government starts to interfere in other matters, such as sheltering aliens and refugees. Your own people first!

However, that means that one is not concerned with the global problems we all deal with, such as peace, security, environmental pollution, etc. The more a government is concerned with national matters, the more we threaten global problems.

That is difficult, especially when we realize that there are 193 (one hundred and ninety three!) sovereign states in this world. States that do not tolerate authority over them, and that decide themselves if and with which other states they would like to cooperate. The substantial problems of the people on earth depend on the willingness of 193 governments, 193 diplomatic services, 193 espionage services, 193 armed forces, and 193, per nation, different cultures, in order to tackle the problems of the world population.

In short, in terms of global cooperation our world is a mess. And it is even worse: we are all unprepared if we want to end the armed conflicts between states, worldwide crime, and acts of terror. No to mention human rights, democracy, and ethics.

The organization of the United Nations is a powerless entity. As such, it is also founded by large powers that either divide their power over the world amongst each other, or quite simply strive for world domination.

There is only one solution for this situation and that is ending the sovereignty of all these 193 states. Retain the right of private policies, of hindering and threatening other countries, of owning their private armed forces, of committing inhumane acts.

And who should govern us?

A world government!

A government that merely focuses on global problems. Because solving those is more important than local problems. Without global authority humanity is left empty-handed.

The Growth of Humanitarianism

One only has to watch the news a couple of times to understand that the idea of a world government did not fall from the sky.

Fortunately, a counter-movement against inhuman behaviour of states and peoples had rapidly developed over the last decades. Here people are at work who are committed to the faith of their fellow human beings, people who do not look at skin colour or other ethnic characteristics. People who are willing to work for everyone, poor and rich, anywhere in the world. The future counts on people who are both humane and think globally. People who like to put an end to all the atrocities the current people inflict on their fellow human beings. People who understand that war, violence, and terror do not solve these atrocities, because all of them bring about hate that causes even more violence.

If we take all of that into account, we may conclude that the world is ready for major political change. The sovereign states should disappear. An army of hundreds of thousands of people is ready to lead humanity in solving political, socio-economic, and ecological problems. If these hundreds of thousands of people would join a political world organization it would be the basis for the joint design of a future filled with lasting peace and humanity. For it we need to concern ourselves with an evolutionary vision. The natural evolution on earth has largely made way for a cultural evolution of the surface of the earth.

Man evolved from being a piece of nature, an animal, into a creature that is more than an animal, to the creator of culture. He has been the initiator, the subject of cultural creation, but is also in danger of becoming its object, its victim.

Man is capable of more than killing fellow human beings. Culture gives us all the possibilities. Man is now called to clearly guide the evolution of culture. How?

By becoming aware of the era in which we live, the Transitium. And by using this era to become aware of all our animalistic traits, to become human and bring forward a humane society. In other words, in order to guide humanity to the Humanium as soon as possible.

To an era of civilisation. To a time of peace, security, equality, and prosperity for all.

However, to do so we need to exchange our existence as a nation for an existence as mankind, a community controlled by a world government.

Violence is never the Answer

There is a dire need for a peaceful world. It does not look like it today. Enmity and violence cause hatred every day. Hate that in itself also causes new acts of violence.

In addition to the regular tense relations between states, the West is plagued by terrorist attacks by individuals or small groups. These are carried out by Islamic jihadists who rely on the Koran. The fact that the attacks are carried out by individuals or small groups proves that, apparently, no State can fight the mighty West. However this situation is currently being questioned due to the (re)creation of the caliphate.

The caliphate is connected to the history of the Islam. The caliphs have always been descendants of Mohammed or his family. There have been many in the course of history. The most famous caliphate was that of the Abbasids (749-1258). It knew two riches, that of Bagdad, and that of Córdoba. The latter introduced Europe in the middle ages to the ancient Greek and Roman civilisations.

In a caliphate the religious ties to the Islam are essential. Nevertheless, the scientific and artistic interests are relatively developed. The Abbasids loved to cite a verse from the Koran saying: 'The ink of a scholar is more sacred than the blood of a martyr.' Caliph Harun ar-Rashid opened the House of Wisdom in Bagdad, where Greek, Persian, and Indian works were studied and translated into the Arabic language. The stories of Thousand-and-one-Night also originate from this time.

The leader of a terrorist group Abu Bakr al-Baghdadi has emerged in the summer of 2014 as a new caliph in the conquered parts of Iraq and Syria. He refers to ISIS as IS, Islamic State. Democracy does not exist in a caliphate. All power resides with the caliph. The caliphate desires to become one large Islamic empire ranging from Iran to the Mediterranean Sea. One does not believe in borders or recognize existing states, not even the state of Israel. That state should disappear. In addition, one also likes to instate the sharia law. Women are required to cover their hair. Adulterous women can be punished with stoning. Apostasy is punished by the death penalty. The same applies to homosexuals. Abu Bakr also introduced a flag for IS. His supporters extent to Libya, Nigeria, and Cameroon (Boko Haram).

Islamic State

However, IS is not the only terrorist group. There are also the Kurds in Turkey who try to ensure that the Turkish government ceases the war against them with attacks. In addition, there are opposing groups in Syria and Iraq who try to reach their goals with terror. The acts of terror are the work of individuals or small groups that can bring about fear and anxiety within a population.

However, the conflicts between the states are more dangerous when it comes to world peace. States have armed forces. Some of them say they possess nuclear bombs. A nuclear bomb offers more possibilities of destroying human beings than terror. A Third World War that was fought with nuclear bombs could, in the end, make it impossible for human life to still be possible.

We have grown accustomed to the fact that in our time violence is the only solution to solve conflicts. It is the survival of the fittest that triumphs. However, violence causes hate and this causes even more violence. Our world is characterized by never ending violence. The large powers and their allies mingle to maintain their power in battle, mostly via aerial bombardments. It resembles a world war in a new form.

A perspective on a peaceful world is missing.

As long as one power, the United States, and its allies own the hegemony of the world power, one will resist this hegemony of the West.

How will it ever come to lasting peace?

By ending all power politics. It is the hallmark of a political system that is based on the principle of exercises of violence, carried out by sovereign states. As long as we tolerate the existence of sovereign states, we will live amongst armed forces that are used to maintain power politics.

Anyone who pursues lasting peace should be guided by the principle that states that the existence of sovereign states comes to an end.

Which government will be able to force sovereign states to give up their sovereignty and take over the government of the world?

A world government.

That government alone would have the power to end all the battles, by making war and violence impossible.

The idea of a world without states emerges today. It is unusual, but therefore not wrong.

The main problem today is how to create such a world government.

This book is dedicated to that problem.

Empathy: Us and the Others

There once was a time when human beings still lived like animals. They lived in small communities with hunters and gatherers, hordes, who lived of the hunt and all the edible products nature had to offer. What kept these people together was the ability to psychologically become one with another member of the hurdle. I call this ability an empathic ability.

Man was a clever animal. Intellect was man's most powerful weapon. He wasn't satisfied with his physical forces, but created artefacts: self-invented and hand-crafted weapons made from wood and stone.

That intellect is what brought people to work together. The hordes formed the group's empathic unit in order to fend off other animals. Thanks to empathic cooperation man was successful in their animalistic existence. Not the lion, but man had become the king of the wilderness.

An example of what the cooperation might accomplish is the following. The horde snuck around a herd of wild horses. Suddenly they, as indicated by their leader, start screaming. The horses feel almost surrounded. They immediately find the only exit and galloped as fast as they can through the gap to escape the angry horde. However, they did not see they were heading towards a steep cliff.

They all fall down and become an easy prey for the celebrating horde.

Man was indeed a remarkable animal. He was a successful animal. However, it also had a negative aspect because more and more hordes would emerge. So many that in the end they had to fight each other for the possession of hunting fields.

From a young age man learned that other hordes stole the food of their own. As a result the horde was forced to become a true battle group. Every member of the horde was prepared to put his life on the line for the horde. No other species can be discussed of which so many members of the same kind fought each other. Therefore, empathy ensures a link between the own group and generates animosity towards the 'others'.

People that belonged to another horde were, as a rule, the enemy. They were enemies because they, in the eyes of the horde, belonged to the 'others'.

Certain feelings that kept the horde together were feelings of empathy. Man possess this feeling without being aware of it. It is the unconscious ability to become one with another. He 'reads', as it were, what the other is feeling. This empathic ability that dates back to the time of the hordes one has kept until this day.

Empathy unites people in order to become a close-knit community. For people outside of the community empathy usually works differently. Any man still possesses, sometimes against their will, his objections to 'others'. How can you tell that they are others? Their language, their customs, their way of living together, their religion, but mostly their appearance. There are still white people that have difficulty with 'niggers'.

In Germany lived the Nazis who knew exactly which peoples had to be eradicated. Because they were 'different'.

In short: a human community is potentially always a battle group when they meet 'others' on their way. 'Others' are enemies.

Existence: From Nature to Culture

Approximately ten thousand years ago man made a great discovery. As long as they functioned as a horde they could live from the hunt and everything edible they found in the jungle.

However, the climate was changing. They had only known the ice age which had forced them to live in caves. Only during the day they would leave their hiding places to hunt for food. However, a time was approaching that would often the climate century by century. They saw how glaciers melted, and how streams of water came crashing down. Low-lying land was flooded. The water level in the oceans rose which resulted in the North Sea, England became an island, and the channel between France and England arose. A large piece of lowland south of Europe flowed with water from the Atlantic Ocean. This became the Mediterranean Sea.

The mythology of all countries talks about this flood: the Flood Myth. However, the people that escaped the rising water enjoyed the mild climate. There were flowers everywhere, insects were buzzing through the air, and woods were formed, in short, the earth became a somewhat idyllic place. And that was when man made the greatest discovery of all time. They discovered that you cannot only acquire food by hunting and gathering, but that you can also produce it. One would collect seeds of grass from a kind that produces considerable seeds, and spread it out on the soil that had been stripped of other crops. Every seed one put in the ground turned into twenty seeds!

During the summer the seeds would be ready to be harvest. And if one had ground enough, with a grinder in a bowl made from dried clay, it could be used to make food over a fire.

However, this did mean one could no longer roam around like a nomad, so man ended his nomadic existence. One needed to build a shelter at the place where there were fields and meadows. That piece of shelter became a home.

That was how the first villages came to be, which were first mainly located in river valleys because that was where the soil was most fertile. The oldest river valleys were the valley of the Nile, and the valley of the Euphrates and Tigris.

Today we claim that one invented culture, or in other words agriculture and also cattle breeding. The latter was clear because the chickens voluntarily walked to the villages and it wasn't difficult to tame cattle. They were moved to a stable.

People's lives were changing. They turned into villagers after having been nomads, after being hunters and gatherers one would become farmers, the horde turned into a village community. Soon one only discussed sowing, harvesting, clothes made from wool, shoes made out of leather, barrels to store the harvest, irrigation, storage of stock, agricultural tools etc.

A greater change was hardly conceivable.

II

The Emergence of the State

Communities begin to Organize

In the villages there was always a lot to do aside from farming. Some people focused on building houses and stables, while others made tools. On the fields one dug and harrowed, on water one fished and used the water for irrigation. Without proper tools one could not do these things.

One retrieved copper from the mountains as a raw material for tools. However, copper turned out to be too soft until someone discovered that it became excellent material if you combined it with tin and fire. The blacksmith made his first appearance. Soon the village population was not only comprised of farmers.

A number of manual workers emerged, but there were also people who guarded the villages day and night. These men needed weapons. There were also priests, who built temples for the gods and goddesses and prayed to them to protect people from floods and other disasters.

It did not take long before the villagers agreed to enable one of them ensure the cooperation between all the groups in the village. This was clear because in the past every horde had a leader. The leaders from old times had demanded obedience of everyone in the fight against animals and human beings. The same would apply to the changed circumstances.

The pharaohs' slaves

The culture became a success. Some villages turned into cities.

After some time such farming cultures developed into what we today call cities. One of the cities became the capital of the state. A hereditary leader became the head of the community. The new leader became the king. After some time the king became a man who far outreached the rest of the community. For instance, in Egypt he became a pharaoh.

In time the pharaohs became some kind of god. Their graves were the pyramids in which one kept the body of the pharaoh, something that had to continue to exist otherwise it would not end up in heaven. One made the body sustainable by embalming it.

The pharaoh had employed people as civil servants and warriors. The priests were relatively independent. In addition, the craftsmen often served the king.

We can say that the warriors were there for a reason because states were often at war. A famous relief has been preserved of the pharaoh holding his enemy up by his hairs and lifting his club to give the final blow.

Many images are preserved in rock and clay and remind us of the numerous wars of the neighbouring state, that of the Assyrian people, who often organized campaigns in their living area, Mesopotamia, to prove their superiority in the war. From the start the state has been an instrument of power and warfare.

This never changed throughout the centuries.

States sometimes turn into Empires

Peoples who were successful in their fights against their neighbours thought they were chosen by the gods to create a large empire. In Europe the first large empire that emerged was the empire of the city of Rome, the Roman Empire. At the same time, approximately two millennia ago, the Chinese Empire emerged in Asia.

In both empires the military played an essential role. They thought strategically. The empire had to be protected from enemies. The borders, a new concept, had to be equipped with forts that were manned by soldiers. In both empires one created an extended protective border on the northern side of the empire. In Europe the Romans were able to use a natural barrier, formed by the Rhine and the Danube River. In China one built an enormous wall. Its remains are still admired by tourists today. In short, every state had a military force, a military force comprised of professional soldiers.

It goes without saying that the soldiers were essential in society. Initially the city of Rome was only comprised of the city. Soon after the Romans conquered Italy, the Mediterranean Basin, and finally the whole of southern Europe.

Rome's language was Latin. Today, Italian, Spanish, Portuguese, French, and Romanian are called 'Romance Languages' because in origin they were Latin and transformed into another language over the course of two millennia.

The State Guards its Ownership

The power of the state was enforced within the territory of the country. A governmental system had to be implemented and rules had to be established for society, laid down in a system of laws.

The oldest inhabitants were often the people with lots of land. Newcomers owned, as a general rule, little or even no land. The cities eldest, the patriarchs, or the rulers, ensured that their ownership of large pieces of land merely belonged to themselves and their descendants.

The main conditions of the law were based on legacy. The oldest son was usually the only person who inherited from his father. This in order to prevent endless struggles between sons.

It went without saying that the women living in the cities were given a low position in the legal order. Their task was strictly limited to giving birth and raising children. However, in the higher ranks they often played a part as the woman behind the scenes.

The government also had to maintain order. The latter wasn't always easy, especially when it came to ethnic minorities among the population of the empire, people from outside the borders who had become inhabitants of the empire because the empire had added their living area to their realm. As such the Romans struggled with the Celts and Germanic tribes, and the Chinese with the Huns and Mongols.

Gladiators in Rome

As the population increased more immigrants moved to the cities. They were poor people. As people who did not own any land, or were unable to own land because of the law there was nothing left to do than report for service at a rich lord. However, a servant had no rights. He became a slave, a famulus. However, as such he did belong to the family of the lord.

That was how society was divided into social classes.

At the top were the rich patriarchs, followed by the newcomers, and at the bottom were the slaves. In ancient Rome one would call the newcomers plebejers. They never got equal rights, they were 'others'.

Occasionally a revolt would break out amongst the slaves who worked for a landowner. Known was Spartacus' revolt.

Some of the slaves became gladiators, sword fighters. They would perform in arenas where sometimes a colourful audience entertained themselves while they slaughtered their colleagues. Let's continue our journey through the Roman Empire. The inhabitants of Rome were villagers who had separated themselves from the rural population. Every city centre was formed by the market. On agreed times the city would open its gates and farmers would enter carrying their produce on carts, often pulled by donkeys.

Initially trade was based on exchange.

The Romans used pieces of cow skin as money. The word pecunia (from pecus = cattle) became the word used for money, even when one already started making coins out of copper and silver. The areas surrounding the cities were transformed from natural areas into cultural ground.

In the meantime trade had also become a means for the farmers to exist, and for villagers to buy food. Many was indispensable in this regard. Over the course of time it became increasingly important. The state guarded its ownership. There were rich and poor people. It had to remain that way, something the patriarchs took care of. As members of the senate they made the laws.

The State Guards its Identity

Let us take a leap into the present. The current states are mainly held together by nationalism. With it I mean the feelings of citizens to feel one, to feel like patriots. There is such a thing as a collective identity of the people that live in the same state.

The current nationalism is a product of Western soil. The Enlightenment (18th century) in Europe was a time of new ideas. It was at that time when one introduced the idea that all people are equal members of society. And they should also be treated as equals in this society, regardless of ethnic or other differences. All people were given equal rights. Initially this principle of equality led to an ideal bond between the people of all the states. For the first time ever the song 'Alle Menschen warden Brüder' was heard around Europe.

Napoleon, raised in the French Revolution (1789-1799) did not feel the same. The French were superior to all other peoples. Napoleon brought a large part of Europe under his authority. Only after his defeat at Waterloo the people from Europe felt freed of his tyranny. From the freedom battle against Napoleon merged the national states, states that were carried by nationalism.

Nationalism puts its own nation first and is often based on the superiority of the nation. The peoples all sing their own national anthem and have their own flag. They reverted to worshipping a father of the fatherland, and the heroes from the history of their fatherland. National holidays were established where one worships the royal house or the father of the fatherland, and enthusiastically sings and parties around the national flag.

Ever since historians have been writing about the birth of their own state, about wars with the enemies, and about the evolution of their own culture. These books are compulsory and all included in educational programs.

If someone at the Olympic Games wins, the flag of their country is risen, and the anthem of his or her country is played.

He or she has brought world fame upon their country. He or she has become a hero. The state carefully keeps the difference between their own citizens and those from other countries. Only their own citizens have the right to own a passport that confirms their nationality. Children from immigrants with a double passport are considered to be a problem.

The State Promotes Nationalism

The state has an interest in seeing that its population feels like one. That is why it promotes national feelings. Something one already stimulates in lower education when one discusses national heroes in history class with the children. The fact that history is violated as such is something one does not care about. If one, as a people, committed crimes in the past little attention is paid to it during history class – or one even denied it happened. In history people step forward as national heroes whose actions one cannot always call humane. It is one of the reasons why history is still a permanent discussion.

In the United States, where the indigenous population no longer plays a role, and where immigrants from many countries are forced to live with others, many classrooms are decorated with the national flag. The government creates the nation. In the United States one is not quickly given their new nationality.

The great number of refugees awaits an unknown fate in the European countries. Will these people continue to live in their new country? Should they all receive the nationality of their new country?

In short, national consciousness is currently problematic.

Populists make use of this situation by saying: own people first!

A next idea could be: all of you out! You are others!

The State Guards its Sovereignty

Today a whole network of states has been cast over the surface of the earth. The current world order is a hotchpotch of states. The General Assembly of the United Nations is currently represented by representatives from 193 states. Striking is the large number of former colonies that have fought for their freedom in the previous century. Many of them do not count in world politics. But there are also large powers (states that have a lot of power), like the United States, Russia, France, the United Kingdom, Germany, India, Pakistan, Indonesia, China, Japan, Brazil, and other countries.

States do not only have a national flag and a national anthem, they also have their own government, their own board, they carry out their own political policy, they have their own diplomatic service, own one or more espionage services, and have their own army, their own armed forces at their disposal. Each state has the right to do so.

Every state is sovereign.

The government (the government of state) is always ready to protect the people, the nation. A good government ensures proper armed forces. There is a field army, a navy, and an air force. Every part of the force has modern weapons at their disposal, the field army has artillery, machine guns and tanks, and the navy has destroyers, minesweepers, cruisers, and aircraft carriers. The latter are connected to the air force, which has fighter aircrafts, bombers, and drones.

And the ideal of every state is owning nuclear weapons. One, when in possession of such weapons, needs to take care of long distance rockets. The possession of nuclear weapons ensures that one as a state, counts in the world.

The army is the pride of the nation. It is a connection between all members of the national community. It is still always a great honour to receive a distinction for services rendered to the home country.

Nationalism and sovereignty stem from the remnants of animalistic feelings. Together they form the fuse that starts world wars.

The State Demands Obedience

The tolerance one promotes in terms of dissidents varies per country. To a large extent this depends on the rulers. The same applies to European history.

In the middle ages the church was a powerful institution. Anyone who disagreed with its explanations of the Christian faith was declared to be a heretic by the inquisition. A heretic often ended his life on the stake.

After the middle ages the modern time introduced itself in Europe which started with a fundamental change in the zeitgeist. Individualism and a critical mind-set were introduced. This criticism was often also aimed at the Catholic Church. Luther was one of the people who led a movement to reform the church. However, this reformation movement led to a separation. From that moment on the Catholic Church saw the Protestants standing completely opposite them. The inquisition couldn't change any of it.

The European Protestants found protection in many states. A war commenced that would last 30 years (1618-1648) and would lead to an everlasting separation in Europe. For peace it was agreed that the ruler of each country would decide which religion was permitted. The result was that the southern states in Europe would be catholic, the northern states Protestant.

Luther

The modern time gave rulers unprecedented power. They enjoyed the freedom of going to war because of their power politics. This lust for power began to play an increasingly important role in European, but, later on, also in global politics. The history of mankind is the history of the lust and struggle for power.

The State Threatens Peace

We learned before that the state is not infrequently the embodiment of power. And that means that the interests of mankind as a whole are ignored. Because mankind merely has global interests, matters that involve the planet as a whole.

Especially large powers desire maintaining or increasing their power. It is some kind of lust for power, especially amongst the armed forces. In the diplomatic game that is played worldwide the state's instruments of power, the government, the diplomatic service, the secret services, and the army, each play their own role. However, it is always subordinate to the power game of the state.

The state only has a leading figure. The statesman who once tasted of the power is often engulfed by it. It is a remarkable thing when people listen to you, if journalists write down every word you say, if the media treats you with respect, if you find yourself in pictures printed in newspapers and magazines, if your legislative proposals are accepted by the representatives of the people, when you are praised for the excellent manner in which you look after the interests of the country.

And it concerns the last one in particular. How one, as a power bearing politician, takes care of the interests of the country. Of course the interests of their own country.

After the Second World War the presidents of the United States established themselves as masters in terms of their lust for power. They organized revolutions in South-America, they made trade with other countries impossible, and the influence of the CIA was felt throughout the word. On the other hand, the Russians made use of the uprising of the colonies. Throughout, both parties' lust for power clashed, however, this time it was publicly displayed.

Power politics rarely lead to war. Prior to it the world population is manipulated by bodies dealing with propaganda that call for violence. The foreign policy of each state is a power game.

The System of States Leads to Armaments

Since the start of the new time (approximately 5 centuries ago) the states in Europe have been desiring large individual armies. The soldiers insist on weaponry that is as modern as possible. Since the invention of gunpowder one transformed the artillery into a weapon that can be used to breach walls. That was how cities could be conquered. But also muskets and the subsequent rifles were significant. Today every modern army has machine guns, war ships, tanks, and planes at its disposal. In short, the potential for murder continues to grow.

The war industry has always been the basis for technical innovation. Technique became more scientific which led to technology. The current universities have become suppliers of technological development that, not infrequently, enables the armaments industry to progress.

Today science and armaments go hand in hand. The science of the smallest subatomic particles brought about the sudden ending of the Second World War. The United States launched two atomic bombs aimed at Japanese cities.

However, the current nuclear bombs have become even more destructive. Mankind is capable of destroying itself.

The danger of a Third World War has emerged. The large states are clearly involved in an arms race. Over the course of time their lust for power has not diminished. In the media commentators explain which oppositions in the current world politics are at play. However, in the end it all comes down to one thing: the desire for power.

War industry

The question arises: should world politics still merely revolve around this? It might have been logical in the time of the Pharaohs, but today?

Back then, ages before Christ, there were only a few states. But how many are there today? Since the Second World War colonies have freed themselves from oppression.

The United Nation has 193 members.

Therefore there are 193 states that have nuclear weapons at their disposal.

I believe there are 193 states too many. If we ever want to end this desire for power we can do nothing but eliminating the system of states. It needs to be replaced by a global governance that puts an end to all militarism.

Militarism does not belong to this day and age. Is has become an anachronism.

Merely a new world order without states can ensure civilisation.

Globalisation

Around 1500 the Europeans began to control the world. Their ships sailed the oceans of the world and a colonisation process emerged, which resulted into the fact that Central and South America adopted the Portuguese and Spanish language as their lingua franca. From these countries colonists stole the silver that became the basis of the financial system.

Initially, Portugal and Spain were leading countries of the Western dominance in the world. Later on their position was taken by countries as the Republic of the Netherlands, France, England, and even later (since the Second World War) the United States of Northern America. It were always the Western countries that took the lead. Historians have called the age from 1500 until today the Modern History.

In this era the power game has controlled world politics. It is still based on the ingrained power politics that has characterizes the relations of the states since the rise of the states in the old times. However, this concept has been outdated for quite some time. Currently the world is involved in a process of 'globalisation'.

Nevertheless, it is all about 'westernisation'. The culture of the West has spread all over the earth. All countries adapt the technology of the West because it is more advanced than in other countries. In addition to the economic and financial bases of the Western economy. A worldwide trade has been established where one makes use of western sizes and weights, where one writes their letters in English, and adapts the Western Gregorian calendar.

The westernisation has evolved quickly. All major cities in the world are built on the same profile of skyscrapers, business sites, trams, buses, subways, shops, factories, offices, pharmacies, hospitals, museums, and educational institutions. Western fashion has conquered the world. In short, the world is rapidly westernizing.

Slavery and colonialism, Namibia

The most significant fact of globalisation is the interdependence of the economic and financial world system. If, in China, an economic depression occurs, all the stock markets in the world are affected by it.

Today, the economic evolution has, after the industrial revolution, produced a new revolution, the Digital Revolution, which has, among other things, expanded and accelerated the international people, and business traffic.

Globalisation is also fed by currents of people moving from the poor to the rich world. Today this current also includes refugees from Syria, Iraq, and other war zones.

Globalisation could be a blessing for the population of the world because it, more than anything, reinforces the realisation that we all live in one world, in the same world.

However, for now it seems that there is more hostility between states than ever before.

It is a shame because the realisation of one world is a prerequisite for world peace.

III

The Final Crisis of the Transitium

Chaos and Inhumanity

It will not be a coincidence if the last age of the Transitium will be the Modern Age. The evolution of culture, as all processes of evolution, experiences times of crisis that on one hand fill society with chaos, but on the other hand can also be the announcement of a new stage of evolution.

Often people do not see the changes that occur, mostly because they occur over larger time units than one might assume. However, if man considers history to be a part of the evolution of human existence, the contours of a new age become visible.

That is when one, for instance, sees the concept of globalisation rise (=westernisation), it is a sign of cultural renewal. That is also when one fully appreciates the Digital Revolution. Let us make a clear distinction between the decay of the old – and the rise of the new.

What is most striking today is how we seem to relapse to an animal-like state, one we still experience after all the chaos and the bloodshed in the last century.

Let me return to the primitive character of our current cultural crisis. I cannot emphasize enough how primitive all culture still is. And it is so obvious. Culture is, evolutionary speaking, after all not a recent invention, not older than approximately 10.000 years.

Ten thousand years is, on an evolutionary scale, very short. You can barely call it an age. Ten thousand years are one hundred centuries. Let us assume that within each century four new generations of man follow each other. This would mean that, since the origin of the oldest cultures, four hundred generations have taken each other's place. Man might have been working for four hundred generations to exchange his animal-like features for humanity. However, it apparently wasn't enough time to completely lose the animal within. Our culture still deals with primitive, animal-like features.

For quite some time scholars have been involved in dissecting culture: sociologists, ethnologists, economists, and psychologists, however, those who study the aspect of culture in its entirety are the historians.

Nevertheless, historians do not think in terms of hundreds of thousands of years. They, as historians, do not reach back to the Animalium, and they do not focus on the Transitium. I do not know a history book in which it was said that all culture is still primitive. Some historians did notice, however, that around 1900 the world society degenerated into a so-called cultural crisis. With it one refers to an age of destruction in blindness, a loss of norms and values, and inhumanities.

I mentioned earlier that the West has had an advantage on the rest of the world since 1500. That advantage also applied to warfare. The military potential, the ability to wreak death and destruction, increased from century to century.

When the twentieth century approached a war commenced the world had never experienced before.

The Bloodbath of the Colonisation of Africa

Man's first great atrocity in the age of the cultural crisis that started around 1900 was the colonisation of Africa.

In the nineteenth century European states had begun to industrialize. The need for raw materials and other natural resources increased. In the 80s and 90s of the nineteenth century a race for the possession of areas filled with raw materials and markets began. Areas such as these were transformed into colonies. Traditionally the United Kingdom owned India and became very active in the east of Africa. The same applied to France which mastered Africa north of the Sahara desert, and large parts of West Africa. In addition to the Germans who were active in East Africa and Namibia. South Africa was annexed in 1910 by the English after the country had functioned as a staging post for the Dutch East India Company since 1652. Other European countries also took part in the colonisation of Africa.

The continent was divided among fifteen European countries and the United States at the Conference of Berlin (1884-1885). At the time Africa did not house peoples, but approximately 10.000 tribes were living in the country. The Europeans divided these tribes amongst each other, 39 European countries, in 1900. The United States was also given a small part of the tribal area intended for released slaves who wanted to return to their origin. The Americans called it Liberia.

In Asia colonisation also took place. In South-East Asia the Netherlands had started the conquest of the Dutch East Indies (now Indonesia) centuries ago. France made itself the master of Vietnam, Laos, and Cambodia. In name China remained independent, however, it became a kind of collective colony owned by the Western countries. Only Japan had managed to maintain its independence in the nineteenth century and followed the West in terms of industrialisation. Japan colonized Korea. The Russians occupied the entire area of North Asia that was called Siberia.

An example of a European colonizer was the Belgian king Leopold II. He crowned himself to be the private owner of Congo in Central Africa, an area of more than two million square kilometres. He considered Congo to be an excellent means for acquiring wealth. He never visited Congo himself but controlled his empire with the help of a large army of mercenaries.

First and foremost he paid attention to ivory and, since 1890, to rubber, of which the price strongly increased. He gave the order that forced the indigenous population to create rubber plantations and collect the juice from the rubber plants.

King Leopold II's 23-year-long reign was characterized by genocide, slavery, abductions, torture, rape, and chopping off hands. One estimates the number of victims ranging from five to ten million.

Rubber plantation Congo

Even though this atrocities were concealed in Belgium the case became a notorious international scandal. In 1908 Leopold felt his end was near. He offered his property in return for a substantial compensation to the Belgian state. He died owning dozens of orders and awards, among which the Cross in the order of the Dutch Lion.

In 1888 he established the Order of the African Star 'as a reward to the independent state of Congo and, in general, the case of the African civilisation'.

Thus, he did not think of humanity when he talked about 'civilisation'. Moreover, that is true for all statesmen who grant awards to people like him.

Conclusion: evolution takes time. Even people today have primitive, animal-like features.

Let us be aware of that.

The Bloodbath of the First World War

The twentieth century turned out to be the bloodiest in history. Never before have so many people, soldiers, and civilians died. It was obvious. The weapons became even more perfect to kill massively.

The history of the twentieth century is sad when it comes to humanity.

It started early on in the century with two World Wars in Europe. The tensions between the major powers soon escalated. An arms race began that, in the First World War, introduced quick firearms, heavy artillery, fleets, and tanks. During the Second World War fighter planes, bombers, and rockets were added to the list.

The same countries that found each other in 1884/85 during the division of Africa started a mutual war in 1914. It was unprecedented for that time: a battle of whites against whites. In addition to it being a battle with many victims.

The large European powers participated in the First World War. It was the question whether the people of Germany would join the fight. After all, Germany was a country where the social democrats enjoyed a dominant position. For instance, there was one party that continuously voted against the war budgets in parliament, it was the SDP. This party could, and would prevent Germany from being dragged into a war, as the socialists expected.

British soldiers, blinded by chemical weapons

However, that wasn't the case. The SDP showed itself to be a nationalist party. On the day of the declaration of war the party leaders called in its newspaper for the support of the emperor to save the country. The socialist who were subject to military service meekly joined the transport to the front. In the German trains one could often hear cheers and people celebrating. All were sure that Germany would be victorious. The great Habsburg Empire was an ally of Germany and Turkey (the centrals). Opposite were countries as France, Great Britain, and Russia, and later on also the United States (the Allies).

After the Germans' smooth progression via Belgium and a large part of France the front was stuck. The war lost its dynamic and, from that moment on, suppressed in the trenches. For four years both parties were laying opposite each other in their trenches. Occasionally soldiers were forced to leave the safety of the trenches and march forward to break enemy lines. Every attempt took thousands of lives and led to stacks of bodies. During the final year of the war the United States stepped in to help the allied forces. In November of 1918 Germany put down its arms. Numbers published after the war count a small five and a half million dead on the side of the allied forces, and over four million on the side of the centrals. In total nine and a half million soldiers. The number of wounded and civilian victims is not included in this number. That was approximately four million.

The League of Nations Clings to the System of States

After the end of the war there were still many people who shared the hope of a better world. There were so many who died, something like that wouldn't be repeated. They hoped for everlasting peace and a renewal of the world order.

The idea of a new world order originated from the American president Thomas Woodrow Wilson.

He introduced, as one of his fourteen aspects of the Treaty of Versailles, the creation of the first supranational organisation, the League of Nations. The head office would be in Geneva, Switzerland. No nationalism, but supra-nationalism: it was truly a new idea. Sovereign states would agree that they would be controlled by an authority they had to obey.

The League of Nations was given the task to create peace on earth. Never before had the concept of a world with everlasting peace been so close.

But it would be otherwise. The American congress refused to sign the Treaty of Versailles. As a result the country did not become a member of the League of Nations or join the supra-national League of Nations.

Now that the instigator was out of the picture the supra-national principle ended up in the trash. As a result, nationalism was far from dead. It was now wrapped up in geopolitical strategies. The United

Kingdom, France, Italy, and Japan became the permanent members of the General Meeting. All these countries belonged to the victors of the First World War. From the start it was clear that they would use the League of Nations for themselves as an instrument of power.

No one ended the system of states. And that was when experts understood that the ancient power politics remained to rule, including the armament, the espionage, the secret diplomacy, and the old political strategy of the desire for power.

In fact, nothing really changed. The world order remained a worldwide nest of power politics. When in the thirties Germany, Italy, and Japan left the League of Nations the new fronts had already been prepped. The arms for the Second World War already began to accumulate.

In 1919 Thomas Woodrow Wilson was awarded the Nobel Peace Prize. He must have understood that when he died (1924) this prize was the only thing he contributed to peace.

A deep hate had taken a hold of the peoples of countries that had participated in the war. The French cursed the Germans – and vice versa. The Belgians were deeply humiliated and had lost many civilians. In 1914 more than one million Belgian inhabitants fled to the Netherlands which had remained neutral. In Belgium heavy battles were fought against the Germans. Many memorials in Belgium remind one of it every day. Today we see similar memorials in France in the areas where one fought the most, at the Marne and at Verdun.

The First World War was a slaughter Europe had never experienced before. There were only a few families in the participating countries who had no one to mourn for.

The harvest of the war was a deep hatred dispersed over entire peoples. The victors shifted their hatred towards the opponents. This became clear at the Peace of Versailles (1919). Peace was imposed. Germany was the loser and had to take full responsibility for the total costs of the war, a pricelessly high amount. A peace treaty cannot be filled with more hatred. It was imposed – without anyone thinking about what the consequences might be. The Germans came up with a trick that would enable them to pay the colossal debt. They allowed the value of the mark to drop to an absolute minimum. It was simple, as long as you produced enough without coverage. In 1923 one had to add a stamp of several million mark to a letter in Germany.

That was when one began to restore the mark.

However, a huge part of the German population had become very poor.

The Bloodbath of the Second World War

It was Adolf Hitler who became very popular with his ideas of revenge. He could benefit from the hatred that had been sown in Germany.

A first attempt to seize power in Bavaria failed, however, the party established by him, the NSDAP (Nazional-Sozialistische Deutsche Arbeiterpartei) became very successful. After a revival of the economy a market crisis occurred at Wall Street, New York in 1929, which led to unemployment and poverty amongst broad sections of the population. Soon the economic crisis began to affect the European countries. The whole of Europe was affected by it.

Hitler saw Mussolini as his example because he had taken over power in Italy shortly after the war. On 30 January, 1933 Hitler did the same in Germany.

Hitler was like a demagogue, a populist. He responded to the feelings of the people he spoke to, something which was very successful in Germany. And he had another trick up his sleeve: not only Versailles would have to pay, the Jews also betrayed Germany. In terms of antisemitism he could use a long history, because Luther had also accused the Jews of great evil.

Hitler could profit from the unemployment when the economic crisis reached Germany. During the elections he became the strongest party. His plan to attack the crisis worked: the country had to spend a lot of money on arms. It was the only way to restart the economy. In September 1939 Hitler started the war with an attack on Poland. This was possible because Stalin and Hitler had concluded a friendship pact only a few days before. Stalin and Hitler divided Poland. Stalin had, by making a pact with Hitler, made the war possible. He counted on Germany and its opponents to kill each other.

However, that was not what happened. In May of 1940 the Netherlands and Belgium were overrun, and in June of 1940 France capitulated. The English quickly left France, but England did manage to withstand the German rain of bombs that followed. Hitler made himself master of the rest of Europe. In 1941 he started his attack on the Soviet Union. In the end this turned out to be a mistake. Despite the death of millions of soldiers and civilians, the Soviet Union remained standing – also because Stalin temporarily suspended his tyrannical rule.

The war turned out to be a true world war because Japan got involved. In 1942 Japan conquered, in a short amount of time, South-East Asia after the American fleet had been destroyed because of a surprise attack from the sky. After the attack the United States decided to join the war as well. After a lengthy conquest of a, by Hitler conquered, part of Russia and Europe, Germany was forced to capitulate in 1945. Hitler committed suicide, but Japan continued its fight. In 1945 this came to a sudden halt. The Americans launched atomic bombs that reached Hiroshima and Nagasaki.

It was the August of 1945 and the war was over.

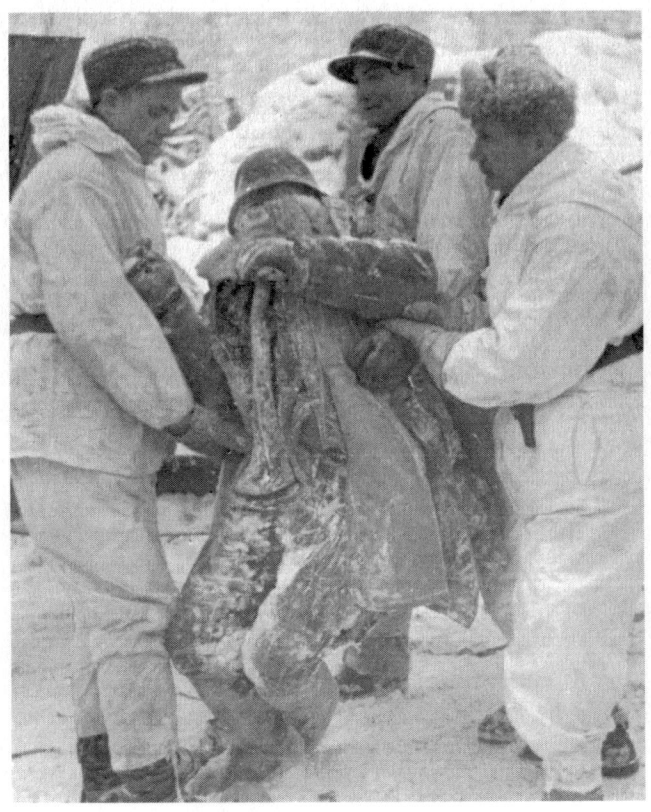

A killed and frozen soldier is buried

Germany was a mess, but the rest of Europe had also suffered a great deal. A lot had to be rebuild.

The total amount of people who died during the Second World War is difficult to quantify, but it is counted at approximately 75 million, among who 50 million civilians and 25 million soldiers.

They are numbers that make the number of victims during the First World War seem like child's play. One can say that both wars were the result of chauvinistic (ultra-nationalist) feelings. However, for the Nazis this also meant that one needed to remove inferior human races from the face of the earth. Hitler had targeted the Jews, Sinti and Roma. The 'Shoah' (Holocaust) was very successful for the Nazis: they were able to kill six million people in the gas chambers, or somewhere else. Never before had humanity been squashed like this.

The end of the Second World War was caused by a new weapon, the atomic bomb. The Japanese cities of Hiroshima and Nagasaki were almost completely ruined, and the population was obliterated. The survivors had to deal with unpleasant consequences. They paid for the aftereffect of the atomic radiation.

We can say that with his atrocity in August of 1945 humanity had reached an ultimate low.

Would there ever be such a thing as humanity in the world?

The worst was to be feared. The Second World War ended with a political situation where two super powers remained who each strived for the hegemony of the earth, the United States and the Soviet Union.

The perverted nationalism had been turned into a battle for world domination. It was power politics pur sang.

The Uno and the Blood Baths in the Rebellious Colonies

After the Second World War the League of Nations was reinstated again, however, it would henceforth be called the United Nations Organisation (UNO). The organisation was useful in many aspects, but, like the League of Nations, was unable to end the system of states, and therefore the threat of war. And it was exactly that, that desire for peace that lived amongst the population of the world.

In the UNO the issue of human rights was discussed for the first time. In the charter of the UNO it was determined that all men, women, and children throughout the world would have equal rights, thus equal rights for a legally fixed treatment by government and private citizens.

On paper the principle of freedom and equality had been reached. The signatories, mostly diplomatic representatives of colonial powers, obviously never hesitated in signing this wonderfully sounding declaration.

Gradually the UNO expanded into an organisation in which all countries participated. Over the course of the twentieth century the colonies all freed themselves from oppression and were allowed to join the new organisation. During the General Meeting all states were given a seat, however, the real power was vested in the super powers, the United States and the Soviet Union. As a result they could continue their battle for the hegemony of the world.

The fight led to an increase of the armament. In 1945 the United States was the only country that possessed an atomic bomb, so the Soviet Union had produce an atomic bomb of their own. In a short amount of time they were successful. The Soviets were also the first to send a satellite into space. Both countries succeeded in keeping each other balanced because of the increase of the armament.

The Soviets supported many countries in South-East Asia in their battle for independence, a battle in which communists often played a role. The Americans ensured counter revolutions that served to establish anti-communist regimes.

This power game has entered history as the Cold War. Once it caused worldwide panic when the Soviets threatened to place atomic rockets on Cuba with which they had close ties.

The United States threatened with atomic attacks if the Soviets did not retreat. They did and that was how the world escaped an atomic war.

First and foremost the UNO was a forum for discussion for diplomats. Whether the diplomats of the large powers energetically dedicated themselves to the question of world peace is something history leaves out.

As a matter of fact they didn't really have the time to do so. They had their hands full with ending the revolts in the colonies. Those foolish individuals thought they could be autonomous. However, after many years of struggle they didn't all turn out to be as foolish as one initially thought…

Vietnam War

The United States and the Soviet Union each 'helped' the rebellious colonies in their own way by establishing capitalist and communist regimes. The help was mostly comprised of supplying arms. That is why the struggle for freedom lasted a lot longer than necessary. When the armed struggle was over (in the 90s the last shots were fired) the colonies were free. However, the Americans ensured that many of the liberated countries became capitalistic with financial support. Sometimes this occurred by means of enormous massacres, like in Indonesia where in 1965 all communists, or those claimed to be communists, were killed, approximately half a million of them. In the background the United States offered a helping hand. Especially in South-East Asia people fought heavily because the French colonies couldn't handle the communist rebels. That was when the United States took over from the French (1957).

Especially the fight in Vietnam was given attention throughout the world. Would the Americans succeed in suppressing this colonized people's desire for freedom with force?

Vietnam was divided into the communist north and the capitalist south. The Vietcong, who controlled the north started his fight in South Vietnam where the pro-Western dictator was in control. The Americans were supported by Thailand, Australia, New Zealand, and the Philippines, but the English and Canadians did not join. The dictator of South Vietnam was impossible. In all the larger cities riots started to break out. Rebellious soldiers occupied Saigon. From that moment on the Americans joined the soldiers.

Under President Kennedy (1961-1963) and President Johnson (1963-1968) the American military's support in Vietnam was gradually increased to more than half a million soldiers. The American air force spread the chemical defoliant called Agent Orange and bombarded rebellious peasants with napalm which is petrol with an adhesive. A photograph of a naked girl trying to escape, still burning because of the napalm was seen all over the world.

As a result many protest songs emerged throughout the entire western world. Boudewijn de Groot wrote 'Weltrusten, meneer de president' (Goodnight Mr. President). The Americans were less and less inclined to burn down houses. The Vietcong won the sympathy of the farmers by dividing the land of the nobles among them. The Americans saw they could no longer win this fight. In 1973 the last of the American soldiers fled a destroyed Vietnam.

The war cost the lives of almost 60.000 American troops.

The Vietnamese counted 2.500.000 million victims.

The Vietnam War gave rise to many protest films with a humanitarian trend, and films that display the madness of the war.

If we assess the impact the UNO has had on world politics we can say that it was close to nothing. The wars continued despite calls made by secretary-generals of the UNO asking for peace.

Not long ago I saw that a victim of the war in Syria begged the UNO to intervene on television. Apparently this man was unaware of the fact that the UNO is an organisation without power, which cannot employ even one soldier.

Finally.

The word humanity is rarely used. It has to do with the fact that it is still difficult to openly plead for a humane society. Therefore it is so difficult because there is no such thing as a worldwide political organisation that stands behind this ideal.

However, the many protest songs and protest films prove that the American population and many people from other countries no longer accepted that soldiers, in an attempt to suppress the historical battle for the freedom of the colonies, made use of napalm and other chemical rubbish.

Nothing has agitated and moved the realisation of how anti-humane a war can be than the Vietnam War.

The Balance of the Twentieth Century

If we take stock of the twentieth century we can see that approximately 170.000.000 (one hundred and seventy million) people died because of another human being.

We still call ourselves, humane, civilized. With 170 million victims in one century I find that slightly exaggerated. Let us admit that we are still ridiculously primitive. It will take some time before we have improved our culture to such an extent that we can speak of a civilisation.

However, we can say that the wars against the battle for freedom of the colonies contributed to an increased awareness of what people focused on until today: killing other human beings. It did bring about a new sense of awareness: the awareness that man is capable of more than murder and manslaughter. And also the awareness that people, all over the world, have the right to live a human life, a humane existence.

In the end the century also brought another surprise with it for the United States and the West. During the last decade of the century the Cold War ended. In 1989 the Berlin Wall fell. De DDR disappeared. All over Eastern Europe revolutions were started against the Stalinist regimes. In the Soviet Union itself matters started to heat up. In 1991 'communism' ended there as well. Germany restored their unity.

In this case it was more than a European matter. A new world order was born. The end of the Cold War because of the disappearance of the Soviet Union brought the world under the control of the United States.

We can say that the twentieth century ended in 1991, not according to the calendar, but in accordance with a new age in the history of mankind. The time when one power controls a world with a heavily loaded past.

Was the United States even aware of the role they would now have to play in matters of world peace and other world problems?

IV

The United States Enforces its Standards on the World

The American World Order

We saw that when we made stock of the twentieth century that a new world order had been born around 1990. It wasn't only the end of Stalinism and the world empire of the Soviet Union, It was also the end of the Cold War.

The United States, supported by its allies, acquired the monopoly on the leadership of the global society.

It was now settled that the future would belong to a capitalist world and its accompanying standards and values on a social-political, and ethnic scale. Democracy would be a priority. A constitution with carefully formulated human rights would adorn any country that wanted to belong to the modern world.

It was the tone of the Western countries, who specifically focused on democracy and human rights. The West, in particular, focused on human rights, the United States in front. To the Americans and Westerners it was clear that their civilisation would be leading in the new world order.

In the book of the American Francis Fukuyama *The End of History and the last man* (1992) the author claims that the end of the Cold War simultaneously meant the end of the struggle for power that characterizes humanity until this day. Peace on earth for man and his capital, humanity moves to its destination: prosperity for all.

No longer the struggle for power, no armaments, no war, the end of the Cultural Evolution is here: the world will, from now on, be guided by the principles of the liberal democracy, that are fixed once and for all.

In short: humanity has reached its final destination.

The American presidents Bush Sr., Clinton, and Bush Jr. made no secret of the fact that capitalism as an economic system, was linked to the standards and values of the West and would apply to the entire world. The United States had shown the world what the ideal society would look like. The only thing the non-western world had to do was simple: follow the American example.

Saddam Hussein's Role

Statesmen are chosen to look after the country's interest. The president of the United States is no exception. First and foremost he needs to focus on internal affairs. Interfering with the rest of the world is an additional task one needs to make time for.

George H.W. Bush, president from 1989-1993 was mostly interested in a third aspect, personal interests. For him these were the oil fields in Iraq. He became acquainted with the royal family of Saudi Arabia and the billionaire's family of Bin Laden.

The relationship with Iraq's dictator Saddam Hussein was more complicated.

Saddam Hussein had played an essential role during the coup of 1968 that brought the Ba'ath party to power in Iraq. The Ba'ath party had a program that was a mixture of nationalism and socialism in an Arabic way. Saddam organized security troops in order to prevent coups.

At the start of the 70s Saddam nationalized an important part of the Iraqi industry. With it the Ba'ath government provided itself with the means to rapidly develop the economy of the country. Power positions in the country were in the hands of the Sunnis, a minority of 20% of the entire population. Saddam Hussein managed to hold on to his power during the war between Iraq and Iran (1980-1988). In Iran Khomeini had come to power who gave the Shiites a revolutionary content. The Shiites would become dominant all over the Islamic world, was his message. With the support of the Arabic States, the United States, and Europe and firmly financed by the Arabic Emirates at the Persian Gulf Saddam became the 'defender of the Arab World against the revolutionary Iran'. Only the Soviet Union refused support him because it prosecuted the communists inside its own borders. Saddam had achieved that he could act as an 'ally to the civilized world'. That civilized world turned a blind eye when it came to his inhumane, violent actions against opponents.

Saddam wasn't able to win the war against Iran despite the aid of the West. West German companies offered him the means and the technique for producing chemical weapons after President Reagan had lifted the export restrictions. The United States also supplied satellite photos where one could see the movements of Iranian troops. Reagan was also able to scratch Iraq off of the list of states that supported terror.

Nevertheless, the war ended in a stalemate. Saddam's Iranian opponents felt they were the ones to carry out a revolutionary form of Islam. They did not give up. During the eight years of the Iraqi-Iranian war hundreds of thousands of people died. Among them were many Kurds and other ethnic minorities living in Iraq who wanted to use the war to free themselves or acquire the equal rights also given to the Sunnis.

In the meantime Iraq had turned into a country that was third on the list of countries being financially supported by the United States.

Saddam Hoessein

The peace of 1988 gave Saddam the opportunity to interfere with Kuwait. If he could get the oil from Kuwait he would own 20% of the world oil reserves (in comparison: Saudi Arabia owned 25%). He demanded that Kuwait would be subjected to the status of an Iraqi province…

It was 1990. The United States had a difficult choice to make. In the meantime it had established proper relationships with the United Arab Emirates at the Persian Gulf. Traditionally it supported Israel. However, when Israel took the side of Kuwait Saddam threatened to wipe half of Israel of the map with chemical weapons.

The American government, led by President George H.W. Bush, attempted to change Saddam's mind by means of diplomacy. The United States, he claimed, obviously did not want to interfere with an internal Arabic conflict. However, he saw no arguments for Iraq to use violence against Kuwait.

When a final conversation between Iraq and Kuwait wasn't solved, the United States made a decision. They refused to continue to support Saddam with his politics. This meant a definitive decision was made to turn against Saddam.

Saddam conquered Kuwait in 1990, but forces of the UNO were established encompassing a number of varying countries as Egypt, Syria, and Czechoslovakia, but mainly comprised of American and English troops. This army drove Saddam's troops from Kuwait in February 1991 (the Gulf War).

After the war President Bush revealed what the American contribution had been to maintain world peace: 'It is a grand idea: a new world order, where different nations are brought together to achieve the universal efforts of humanity: peace and safety, freedom, and obedience to the law'.

What happened in Iraq after the Gulf War?

Social and ethnic unrest arose among the Shiites, Kurds, and rebellious soldiers, however, Saddam succeeded in ruthlessly suppressing all the riots. The rebels did not receive help from the outside world, and Saddam continued his reign.

However, Saddam did more.

His message of Arab nationalism and his call for an Arab unity, autonomy, and social justice spread to many people in the region.

In short, he changed his image from a cruel suppressor to a man who supported Arab nationalism, someone who was against the imperialism of strangers, who, after all, did not shy away from intervention and occupation.

Saddam did even more. From that moment on he posed as a religious follower of the Islam. In his handwriting the following words were added to the Iraqi flag 'Allahu Akbar'. And some elements of the Sharia were added to the Iraqi legislation.

The Americans were able to convince the UNO to impose 'no fly zones' on Iraq because they violated the border with Kuwait. Former CIA agent Robert Baer reported that he had tried to organize a military coup against Saddam Hussein for a decade, and that he had plotted an attack on him in 1995. However, it turned out to be very difficult to eliminate him. President Bill Clinton ordered the attack on Iraq as soon as it ignored the 'no fly zones'. American complaints about the banning of UNO inspectors when it came to suspicious weapons were a pretext for missile attacks in 1997 and 1998. Air raids were carried out in the vicinity of Bagdad in February of 2001.

In February of 2003 Saddam was interviewed by American journalist Dan Rather. He once again denied having used forbidden weapons and claimed that he liked to have a live televised debate with President George W. Bush (2001-2009). He refused. When in March of 2003 forces led by the United States entered

Iraq they hardly met any resistance. Iraq was given a pro-Western regime.

On 5 November, 2006 an Iraqi court found Saddam guilty of violating human rights. He went into hiding but was found. Pictures of him were printed in newspapers. Pictures that showed a dirty refugee with a black beard. On 30 December 2006 he was hanged. A video of his hanging reached the news, where one could hear how Saddam was being yelled at. This led to worldwide turmoil. Later on the head of the guard states that Saddam's body was mutilated with a knife six times after his execution.

Saddam's last letter 'To the great nation, to the people or our country, and humanity', became famous. In this letter he claimed himself to be a chaste man and he called for people not to hate, because hate does not enable one to be honest and it makes you blind, closes all doors to thinking, and keeps you from reasonable thinking, or making the right choice. 'God has given you the ability to become an example of a loving, forgiving, and fraternal coexistence. I also call on you not to hate the peoples of the countries who attacked us. Any who shows remorse – in Iraq or somewhere else – is someone you need to forgive.'

The Americans omitted little to humiliate him and portray him as an evil man. It seems to me that the peoples of the Arab countries did not really accept this. Anti-Western feelings increased.

I think it is likely that this was one of the reasons for the terrorist attacks that followed in the years to come.

The Islamic Radicalisation

Since the 70s the Arab world was unsure how to act against the mighty West. The events in the 90s did not end this. On the contrary. The anti-Western sentiments developed even more than the pro-Western sentiments. In the United States a new child from the Bush-Dynasty had become president, Bush Jr. (2001-2009).

Anyone who had tracked the events in the Islamic world weren't surprised to learn that individuals and groups felt called to act against the Western predominance in the Middle East, and against the Western attitude of superiority. The first terrorists emerged. The twenty-first century started ominously with the well-planned attacks on targets in the United States at 11 September 2001. More than three thousand people were killed. The responsibility was generally attributed to the billionaire Osama bin Laden, the leader of the Al Qaida.

Things between the West and the Islamic world would never again improve. The American world hegemony of the world couldn't have started the twenty-first century any worse.

The terrorist attacks of 9/11 did determine the foreign policy of the new President George W. Bush. He introduced the Bush doctrine: we will not make a distinction between terrorists and those who provide shelter for terrorists, anywhere in the world. Based on this conviction the United States started a war in Afghanistan with massive troops against the Taliban regime that sheltered Osama bin Laden. He had moved to Pakistan where he lived in a spacious villa for ten years. He was invisible here. However, on the orders of President Obama he was tracked down. It was 11 May 2011. He was riddled with bullets by the American commands, even though he wasn't armed. His body was never showed because it was completely deformed, as the media later declared, with more than one hundred bullets. Afterwards one criticized that he wasn't arrested, despite the fact that he wasn't armed. Now it was impossible to carry out a public process. He was thrown into the ocean by the American soldiers who had done all sort of things to his body. It cannot be expected of soldiers, who were trained for special tasks, to behave humanely.

Such behaviour will indeed also occur with 'normally' trained soldiers. A soldier does not focus on humanity. He certainly has something else to do.

The Arab World in Motion

The United States had established its power in the Middle East. American troops guarded Iraqi oil fields. Iraq had a pro-Western regime and at the same time the Americans could count on the support of countries from the region, such as Saudi Arabia, and the United Emirates.

In 2010 a number of uprisings began in the Arab world.

The Western ideology of protesting against everything the government demands of you had reached the Islamic world. The 'Arab Spring' commenced. In the squares of the large cities in Tunisia, Egypt, Libya, and Yemen masses came together to try to force the tyrannical leaders who had ruled over them, to leave. In Syria this turned into a civil war, in Bahrein large demonstrations were organized, in short, the entire Arab World had been set into motion. The reason varied per country: suppression, corruption, a lack of political freedom, and unemployment.

The governments, mostly effectively supported by soldiers, forcefully struck back. One estimates that the number of casualties during the suppression of the Arab Spring ran up to 250.000 in total. What all these revolts had in common was the fact that one blamed the governments for the abuses one opposed.

Arab Spring

To the disappointment of the West the 'Spring' was followed by a radicalisation that spread worldwide. Everywhere in the world women emerged wearing head scarfs, the imams emphasized a woman's responsibility toward her husband, educational institutions refused to allow women who did not wear a headscarf, gays were prosecuted, and the free press did not stand a chance. Occasionally one talked about introducing the sharia law. It didn't matter whether the new leaders were soldiers or citizens, the radicalisation of the Islam was key. The radicalisation always went hand in hand with a growing anti-Western persuasion.

That was obvious.

The only thing with that placed the Islamic world opposite West was the expressions of orthodoxy. Their world had never experienced a time like the enlightenment and even less the fight for the emancipation of women and gays, and something like the reconciliation of the pillars as had occurred in the Netherlands.

In short, the Islamic world had not developed as the West in terms of the evolution of culture. However, by re-introducing old tradition and attributing them to the Koran the Muslims could describe the liberties of the West as the decline of morals.

So now you know, reader, the West is evil, its management of the world is a disgrace for humanity, a good Islamic individual should turn against the West.

Iran was the Shiite country that, in terms of orthodoxy and anti-Western affinities, was the worst in this respect. It suffered because of the Western restrictions on import and export.

And, in secret, it worked on the manufacturing of an atomic bomb, Western media claims. The intervention of the United States and its allies with the Islamic World mostly came down to punishing expeditions in countries that offered shelter to terrorists, first in Afghanistan, the country controlled by the Taliban. The American army had its hand full. They failed in expelling the Taliban. America was the leader of the world. However, more and more it seemed that it controlled the world of the West and its allies.

The presidents of the United States thought they were responsible for not standing in the way of the choice between national and global interests. A 'mission impossible'.

It may be clear for those who face the problem: national and global interests cannot be united.

The world asks for more than the hegemony of one state. Humanity is asking for one global authority which only focuses on their own global interests.

V

Terror and Anti-Terror

'The War on Terror'

It was the term that President George W. Bush used to describe the actions of the United States that followed the eruption of terrorism after 9/11 in 2001.

Bush gave all countries a choice: 'Either you are with us, or you are with the terrorists.' As leader of the world he did not accept a neutral attitude. He considered the attacks to be a declaration of war on the States and its allies. The NATO fully supported him. The West felt itself situated against the rest of the world, and that turned out to be most of the Islamic world. The existing conflicts in Iraq, Chechnya, and the Middle East were now included in the fight against terrorism.

George W. Bush issued a large number of measures that were all intended to discover potential terrorist targets, and increased the power of the government to discover and track terrorist. Nevertheless, attacks occurred all over the world, from Indonesia to Europe. It brought the Western nations together in the fight against Islamic terror.

However, apparently the Westerners didn't see clearly enough that the Islamic world considers the West to be its enemy.

The Americans controlled Iraq via a pro-Western regime, however, the political situation was one filled with continuous revolts against the government. The Sunni regime had to maintain itself against a large majority of the Shiite population. It gave Iran the opportunity to get involved in the conflict. However, there were also ethnic and religious minorities that rebelled. The West, which had learned something from the unsuccessful actions in Afghanistan, did not send troops but helped with aerial bombardments. Radical Muslims dispersed the fight to Syria. The opposing groups, supported by aerial bombardments from the West and Russia, led to a permanent civil war. The West and Russia were both unable to end the civil war in Syria with their support. Syria turned into a country that is dealing with a permanent civil war.

The terrorist movement expanded. On 29 June 2014 a caliphate was established called the IS, or ISIS. Abu Bakr al-Baghdadi appointed himself to be the caliph. He is a well-known terrorist linked to Al Qaida. As caliph he claims religious, political, and military authority over all Muslims. All existing groups based on the Islam are declared unlawful if the troops of the new caliphate emerge. The IS does not shy away from any form of violence and openly displays it on television where they show how one beheads people. Except from Iraq and Syria the IS is active in African countries. The IS is a textbook example of completely drowning in the pool of inhumanity

What is the purpose of the re-establishment of the caliphate? As long as attacks are carried out by individuals or groups of terrorists they solely act on their own authority. They can bring about fear, however, legally speaking they remain criminals.

IS acts as if it is a state. Then one can send terrorist as soldiers of a power. The West couldn't care less, but it is slightly different for the Islamic community.

Many terrorists act as citizens of a state in the making.

But there is more to it. There was a time, in the middle ages and even later on, when the caliphate was a power of authority. Quickly the IS grew out to be a power that influenced Iraq, Syria, Libya, and Nigeria, but the organisation is also active in other areas.

Western countries consider the IS to be a terrorist organisation and approximately 60 countries are directly or indirectly at war with the caliphate. The version of the Islam that supports the IS is the strictly orthodox Salafism. One cannot escape the impression that this reaching back to orthodoxy dispenses an alibi to terrorize the West, which, after all, approves of homosexuality and a number of other reprehensible humane thoughts. It is one of the reasons for the continuing support of the IS for terrorist attacks in Western countries.

Paris and Brussels experienced this recently.

Civil War and Refugees

The chaotic situation of violence that originated in Iraq and Syria is aggravated by the struggle between the Sunnis and Shiites, and the fight for their own territory fought by the Kurds and other ethnic and religious minorities. It is a highly critical situation in areas that are closed off from the world and where famine increases.

In addition, Syria has become the target for a game of power politics for the major powers the United States and Russia. They do not have people on the ground but they bomb the IS from the sky on a daily basis. The question is if supporters of the IS are always the victims. The population as a whole are the ones who are suffering. City after city is destroyed. In countries that are so severely affected by war and violence there is only one thing left to do for most of the population: run.

In 2014 more than one million Iraqi people fled the violence, and in 2015 the number of refugees from Syria reached four million. Most of them found new homes in the neighbouring countries. However, there were also hundreds of thousands of people who tried to find a safe haven a little farther away from home, in Europe where there is no war and a higher level of prosperity.

In Syria the situation has become chaotic, especially because of the aerial bombardments. The population does not have another choice but to try to avoid the danger by escaping to safer resorts. Neighbouring countries Lebanon and Jordan are already filled to the brim with refugees. Via Turkey and Greece one tries to reach Europe.

For most of these refugees the escape to Europe has become a major disappointment. This applies in particular to the high percentage of highly educated individuals among them who, at the time, opted for democracy. The vast majority of them want to go to Germany where Chancellor Angela Merkel once said: 'Wir schaffen das.'

Influx of refugees

The European governments have not demonstrated humane sentiments towards the refugees, except from Chancellor Angela Merkel. From day one Hungary has banned refugees by placing large fences at its borders. The Balkan countries soon did the same. The eastern countries of the European Union also refuse to accept to take but one refugee. The western countries struggle with the refugees.

The problem threatens to divide the European Union because one, more or less, reinstates their own national borders, a result of the fact that the different governments close their borders with fences and installing a strict check at the borders. Sometimes the refugees attempt to breach the fences, but meet soldiers on the other side.

Humanity is not a strange concept for most of the Europeans. However, the governments do not express the same sentiment. This is logical because they are afraid of losing a substantial part of their supporters during elections to the populists. A group of people who, in all openness, call for the ancient feelings of rejecting 'others'. One does not wish to accept 'others' in their own country, because 'others' are enemies. Look at how unreliable they are when they have a chance to assault European women.

The politician who wants to win votes in Europe has little choice: he becomes a populist before he will lose his voters to populism, or he supports the populist program in practice – under the maintenance of the party slogans that are dedicated to a different policy.

According to many Chancellor Angela Merkel made a massive mistake by saying 'Wir schaffen das'. This did not affect the refugees. However, every day more of Merkel's supporters turn against her. Populists reap profits from the arrival of so many 'others'. Feelings once considered to belong to the past relive, feelings that perhaps didn't even leave in the first place. The 'others', they will always be the enemy. The European Union attempts to force Turkey into accepting the non-Syrian refugees for payments and other promises, and take them back from Europe.

There is no global organisation that ensures order in the chaos of the Middle East which is the reason why people escape. The aerial bombardments are, on the one hand, carried out by the United States, and on the other by the Russians. Both powers try to increase their influence in the region. In the absence of leniency between the White House and Putin, Europe will have to ensure peace. However, for now one is busy trying to keep the number of refugees to a minimum by trying to make a distinction between people who have fled because of the war and prosperity seekers. Like the rest of the world Europe is just as exemplary when it comes to the lack of humane behaviour. It makes one think back to the bastions of empires in poor districts.

There are so many millions of refugees, at least there will be as long as one does not deal with the reason why people flee.

However, by securing their borders the European Union is digging its own grave.

VI

Counter-Movement:
Growth of Humanity

From Chaos to Renewal

Since approximately 1900 the world has fallen prey to the deterioration of humanity. Until now we have merely discussed a society in which one diligently kills their fellow human beings with millions at the time. Such a society does not adhere to the most basic of all conditions for humanity, namely not killing each other.

If one already finds it so difficult to adhere to this it is proof of the fact that he has, until now, found it very difficult to overcome his animalistic past.

The scientific understanding in man and culture falls short of the one-sided enthusiasm for the development of technology. The nuclear bomb is the final word of the scientific (and political) world to solving the global cultural crisis we find ourselves in.

Since the victory of capitalism in the 90s of the previous century the standards and values of the capitalist world have become decisive for what is called a 'civilisation'. However, the fast train towards civilisation was hindered on its way due to the outbreak of the financial crisis in 2007 that expanded into the economic crisis in 2008. One that was felt throughout the world.

The existing cultural crisis is intensified by it – or is the economy not a part of the culture? I consider it to be an inevitable part of the cultural crisis today. For a time it appeared as if money grew on trees. However, one by one the banks went belly-up. The governments were unable to maintain the high costs of the banks which led to immense public deficits.

Over the course of the twentieth century the Western world has established a system of care in many countries. In order to save the banks the governments were forced to reduce government spending. It was exactly that carefully constructed health care system that had to make compromises in many countries. Today the financial crisis and the impoverishment brings many people in financial trouble. A small country as the Netherlands has been burdened with 600.000 unemployed individuals for years.

On the other hand, the number of millionaires increases rapidly. They can profit from the economic course taken by the Western countries. That course is also known as neo-liberalism.

President Reagan of the United States and Prime Minister Margaret Thatcher from the United Kingdom promoted it. Neo-liberalism has taken a hold on the capitalist world order. This means that the United States, the European Union and the IMF control the world economy. The market is elevated into an Omni-instrument for growing prosperity. In addition to major industries that work for the market, one has individualized a large part of the governmental services and many semi-public organisations such as housing corporations, education and healthcare institutions. The new owners determine their own salaries and have the opportunity to set up megalomaniac plans for clusters and extensions – that too often go awry.

A cultural crisis is often also accompanied by the decay of standards that traditionally applied to social interaction. The media devote a great deal of attention to phenomena such as corruption, counterfeiting of signatures, theft, tax evasion, doping, silencing letters, and other forms of white-collar practices. A cultural crisis also includes an increase in crime, like killing protected species, taking rich people hostage, trade in ivory, drug trafficking etc. Today there are entire countries that are governed by drug cartels, apart from the old mafia gangs.

All these developments lead to an increase in the gap between rich and poor. The poor are basically left to fend for their own because the workers associations sort of became extinct in the golden 90s of the previous century.

However, the worst aspect is that in a neo-liberal world human relationships become business-like. The same applies to the relationship between governments and its citizens. In a business-like world there is barely room left for humanity. There is no room for peace. The entire Middle-East is on fire. Refugees are traded as livestock by smugglers. Governments obstruct their road at the borders. There are even countries that only grant access if the refugees are willing to hand over their valuable possessions. In some countries one is willing to grant access to refugees, but only in dribs and drabs. The world society is swallowed by corruption and crime, but mostly by a lack of humanity.

A way to solve this cultural crisis is lacking. In other words: a perspective for the future is absent.

An arms race between Europe and Russia is underway, the power struggle continues, and world peace is in danger.

Finding yourself on the path towards peace is the first condition for the survival of humanity. First let us secure world peace.

How?

By digging deep within to the, despite everything, growing humanity.

Pleas for Humanity

The humanity idea dates back to the 19th century. The concept of equality and equal dignity of all human beings was a basic principle of the Enlightenment. The idea is accompanied by a sense of solidarity for 'the others'. Anyone who knows these feelings is someone we can call a humane human being. It goes without saying: humanity is always solidarity.

One of the first signs of emerging feelings of humanity was the abolition of slavery, which occurred in the second half of the nineteenth century. The abolition was not merely a matter of solidarity, economic considerations also played a role. In the United States, during the civil war (1861-1865), where the abolishment or the continuation of slavery was at stake, the capitalist north was opposing the pre-capitalist south. In other countries the rise of capitalism was the cause of the abolition of slavery.

However, at the same time one could also count, among the abolitionists, people who argued that it was also the result of humanity.

A book that focused on the latter and raised global awareness for humanity was *Uncle Tom's Cabin*, written by Harriet Beecher Stow and published in 1852. In the Netherlands a book with similar ideas was published in 1860, titled Max Havelaar written by a man who called himself Multatuli. It was a famous humanitarian indictment. It deals with the exploitation of the inhabitants of the Dutch East Indies. This often occurred via the practices of the indigenous monarchs.

Multatuli's words were compelling. He claimed the king of the Netherlands was responsible for the exploitation. Later on the book became a best-seller. As time passed more translations became available.

Another book belongs to this range, *Das Kapital* written by Karl Marx, the founder of communism. Marx' words bear witness of the emotions of the exploited workers of the 19th century. They are writings particularly prone to the idea of solidarity, humanity, the very beginning of all humanity.

A Humane Attitude towards Animals

I was still a child when I witnessed first-hand how people treated animals. The chicken farmer, at whom my father had arranged for his family to stay for the holiday, occasionally butchered chickens. First he caught them in the chicken coop. The animals tried to escape his grasping fingers in fear. After he had caught about twenty of them and put them in a box covered with gauze he walked outside, where he got them out one by one and snapped their necks. There they lay, twitching. Subsequently he dipped them into a bucket with boiling water. That was how he quickly got rid of their feathers. They were ready for their trip to the poultry plant.

What struck me as a child was how the chicken farmer handled dead material. Nothing made it appear as if, after months of feeding and taking care of them, he had established a bond with the animals. When a small company of people outside for a walk, including his son of eight, caught a frog on their way, the son bit off its head while it was still alive. Ah well, it must be his age, you might say.

Today, the competition demands the rearing of poultry, and pigs, the construction of mega stables in which there is little room for the animals. In addition, the slaughterhouse isn't always a sight for sore eyes. No wonder that, as a result, many today decide to not eat meat.

Bio-industry

Gradually I began to understand that adults sometimes torture an animal with pleasure. I read about cock fights on Java, and about bull fights in Spain. A bull is poked by horsemen as long until he becomes too tired in his attempts to fight of his attackers. That is when one makes room for a hero: the bullfighter who kills it.

We must be grateful for Jane Goodall who introduced us to a humane attitude towards animals. There is nothing wrong with giving primates a name and acknowledging their personality as a result. She argues for one to immediately stop hunting for pleasure. Thanks to her, animals in zoos have much better lives: one gives them inspiring surroundings, based on their nature. However, in Africa many animals suffer from hunting safaris. Elephants have nearly become extinct. Rhino's await a similar fate. In parts of Asia their horns are considered to be lust enhancing. They attract people who desire to become rich quickly.

Today one has reserved game parks in the jungle where it is prohibited to hunt. The fact that it still occurs is the result of many corrupt guards. A lot of money can be made from the ivory of two elephant's teeth.

In Spain bullfighting is an ancient tradition, a fixed part of the national culture. However, over time the objections increased. A more humane attitude towards animals is proven by the fact that gradually there are more people who turn their backs on bullfighting.

In 2012 bullfighting was prohibited in Catalonia. Let's hope the rest of Spain will follow soon.

The Peace Movement

Some realized that the arms race in Europe that started in the 80s of the 19th century could have pernicious consequences. Technology developed rapidly and was quickly introduced in the war industry. The potential of murder kept increasing. It was a woman, Bertha von Suttner, who called on men to end the eternal longing for violence. She was a supporter of Darwin's theory of evolution which he published in a book when he was sixteen years old. She believed that the warmongering man would evolve into a more peace-loving king. However, how do you stimulate such a development? Her experiences in the Caucasus during the Russian-Turkish war, which she reported on as a journalist, had taught her enough about the atrocities of war for her to become a convincing pacifist, something she would remain the rest of her life.

In 1889 Bertha published the pacifistic novel called *Die Waffen nieder!* Her book would have 37 editions and was translated into twelve languages. In this book she clearly describes the atrocities of the war. A lot of people praised her, however, one could also see how difficult it was to go against the sins of your own time. Nevertheless, it never stopped her from writing articles and giving lectures on peace problems. In several countries she took the initiative to establish a peace movement.

Her program consisted of the establishment of an Internal Court of Arbitration. States could present their differences to this court without immediately going to war. And she was successful. In 1899 governmental representatives met in The Hague for the first Peace Conference. Indeed it was decided that one should established a Court of Arbitration. This was later on confirmed in the Peace Palace in The Hague, for the construction of which Carnegie donated the necessary amount of money. However, the Court could not prevent warmongering states from going to war.

The perceptive reader will have discovered that three women played an essential role in three aspects of the newly awoken humanity. Could it be a coincidence?

Defense against the Maltreatment of the Planet

Indeed, you can see that man has taken possession of the earth. Everywhere you will find traces of human habitation. Cities, villages, fields, meadows, orchards, plantations, airports and seaports, railway stations, railroads and car lanes, factories, offices, apartment complexes, masts etc.

All of it rapidly develops, in other words, quickly evolves. This evolution was already present before the Homo sapiens appeared on earth, but that was natural evolution. And today one continues this evolution, but based on its own discretion and at a stunning pace. Evolution has transformed from natural evolution into cultural evolution. Man often brings a halt to natural evolution to make room for culture.

Profound differences have emerged between nature and culture on earth. It resembles a struggle. Nature has to make way for the success of culture.

One would do well to recognize that it is man who continues evolution and is therefore responsible for the further fate of the planet.

A sense of responsibility is an aspect of humanity.

The same applies to the unwanted consequences of the cultural evolution: global warming, the pollution of soil, groundwater, the seas and oceans, the use of soil resources, running out of energy and clean drinking water, the extinction of plants and animals, the absorption of soil resources for the industry, burning down forests to make room for plantations.

The pollution of the sea is shocking. Large ships that carry containers use the cheapest fuel. Yes, well, that competition… That cheap stuff pollutes on a massive scale. It cannot be recommended to drink water from the ocean. A perspective on improving the situation is missing. The earth changes every day. The shift from natural evolution to cultural evolution continues to increase.

And each day the earth becomes more polluted.

Ah well, who will stop these polluters?

Rapid Growth of Humanitarian Organisations

Over the last decades, especially after the Vietnam War, the humanitarian efforts have experienced a turbulent evolution. Aid to victims of natural disasters, starvation, children in need, epidemics, a lack of education have increased. In addition, organisations have been established to protect human rights, others against torture, and organisations for the recovery of victims of armed conflicts.

It is no longer merely a private initiative, help is also offered by NGO's (Non-Governmental Organisations) that are sponsored by governments or funded by the UNO. Thousands of people work for the on aid targeted organisations. Today millions of dollars are supplied by these organisations. Names such as the Red Cross, Doctors without Borders, Oxfam International, Warchild, are mentioned in the media on a daily basis.

It is remarkable that in this sector the work has always had an international character. Humanity does not work with borders!

However, caution is needed in war zones. It can occur that Boko Haram gains control over food supplies and other useful stuff.

Notorious is the case of Ethiopia in 1984. Pop singer Bob Geldof organised a massive concert and raised tens of millions of pounds for the people starving in Ethiopia. And what happened? Dictator Haile Mengistu said 'Thank you', and used the money to continue the fight against Eritrea, Somalia, and the national guerrilla. Oxfam international brought food to the inhabitants of the territory occupied by the rebels. Mengistu ordered the deportation of 600.000 people from the area. Deprived of food and water approximately 100.000 people died during the harsh trip to another territory. Well intended work does not always lead to good results.

It is a shame that these organisations, who do great work, continuously specialize in a certain area of expertise. It is obvious that specialists act together. However, to my knowledge one works closely together.

And yet, it is something that has to be done if we want to save our planet.

VII

Evolution and Progress

Evolution as Leading Concept

Dear reader, the diagram at the beginning of this work already makes it clear that evolution is a leading concept in my work. The diagram reaches back hundreds of thousands of years to the Animalium, in which man lived like animals. However, the diagram also unveils another thought, one of progress. Together they determine the future of man as I see it now: a future of a humane society, the Humanium. The ten thousand years in between are nothing more than a short transitioning period.

Historians limit themselves to a more static approach. They do not recognize the evolution in the course of culture. They describe the fate of people and states, events that occurred within the Transitium. What happened before is the Prehistory, the research area of the prehistory. History is therefore concerned with civil societies, societies in which the formation of state has taken place. The fact that these societies do not always behave humanely is, since the Second World War, the topic of many considerations. An evolutionary approach, as is used in this work, thus makes use of much longer terms and much wider contexts. And this approach creates a different picture of human existence than appears in history. Evolution also means progress.

The cosmos displays changes that have been at play for billions of years and that tantamount to the creation of the continuous increase of opportunities. To use the words of Hubert Reeves: 'In essence man is connected to everything in the universe; he 'originates from the primate, the primate from the cell, the cell from the molecule, the molecule from the atom, the atom from the quark. Our origin lies in the big bang, in the heart of the stars and in the immensity of interstellar space.' (Hubert Reeves, *De Evolutie van het Heelal,* Amsterdam 1986). It revolves around an ascending line: the creation of new opportunities. Evolution occurs step by step: from a state of chaos in which the existing possibilities are depleted a new reality emerges with new possibilities.

One can also find this step by step evolution in the evolution of culture. Dutch historian Huizinga acquired great fame in the 30s of the previous century with his work *Herfsttij der Middeleeuwen.* He describes how everything in the middle ages that was considered to be a virtue such as honestly, loyalty, obedience, tradition, and faith, had to make room for chaos filled with a loss of standards. The book was published in Europe during the rise of Hitler and the Nazism. The parallel was obvious. His student Romein objected to Huizinga's work. He claimed that the book was too one-sided because it only emphasized the aspects of the downfall of the middle ages. It ignores the fact that in that same period a basis was formed for a new age that, under the name of the Renaissance, would bring glory to Europe.

Romein discovered a fixed pattern in the step by step development of culture. Every single time a time of chaos and decay leads to a new time of revival. This revival consists of the growth of new possibilities, of new potential.

He created a 'Law of Increasing Potentiation'. His colleagues did not believe in this historical pattern or in any historical pattern in general.

One can understand this criticism. The law is comprised of much more than culture, it is valid for reality in general. It is the main characteristic of cosmic evolution. Human culture is also subject to this law.

Since approximately 1900 a chaotic time occurred in culture, a time of blood baths and of the collapse of humanity.

However, at the same time we also experience how more people became active to ensure a better world, one that is peaceful and humane.

It can only be hoped that they find each other globally, and establish a global organisation to preserve the planet, culture, and man.

A world that will be guided by a world government.

What could a World Government do?

The system of states is the embodiment of the political world order. Until today this system has led to disaster, war, and a waste of earthly resources. The system was established many centuries before the start of our calendar. It survived itself and became an anachronism. The current world requires a different political order. In order to control the current society a world government is required.

Have you ever thought about this?

A world government would not be responsible for guarding the interests of a state or a group of states, but those of humanity.

It is possible if one eliminates all 193 states. In other words: if one strips them of their sovereign rights. One is no longer entitled to control a board that is mainly focused on its own private interests, or entitled to their own armed forces.

This dismantling of sovereignty of the existing states would result into the subordination of private interests to the demands of the global government. The states would become 'provinces' or 'departments'.

This would give the global governance, the world government, the opportunity to abolish all armed forces, dismantle all weapons, in the first place the atomic weapons and missile installations, all tanks, fighter planes, naval ships, and carefully disassemble ammunition arsenals, to close all barracks, end all military training, and prohibit the trade in weapons made for war. In other words: to make war impossible.

The billions of money annually spent to armament could be used by the global authority.

The first task of the global authority would be to establish a constitution in which it is stated that all people on earth, men, women, and children, possess equal rights, despite their ethnic background or otherwise.

It will state that based on this principle all people on earth have a right to the equal distribution of prosperity. This would mean that everyone can have shelter, food, and drinking water, medical care, and education.

Thus, the first task of the world government would be to end the differences in wealth between the regions on earth. The equalisation of wealth would end the increase of millions of migrants.

In short, the borders will be abolished. There will no longer be rich or poor countries, wealth will be fairly distributed. It is time for extremely poor countries to fade, where people have to walk for hours to obtain some water, where medical facilities do not exist, where there is no such thing as education, and where people are extremely happy if they only have something to eat.

The economic conditions are in place to enable all people on earth to share in their wealth. The world government should have sufficient resources for it. That is why they will become the owner of the soil recourses of the earth, which they will make available and distribute to the needs of each region. A world government will carry out its plans to put an end to all ecological problems, such as climate control, the pollution of the environment, the stock depletion of oceans, and the preservation of wildlife. The world government will introduce global discussions about how society should be organised. The world government will provide all citizens of the world with the democratic rights a modern society needs. The world government will enable anyone to get access to all the education one might need. However, most importantly: the world government will ensure a humane society that is based on solidarity, that is to say a society in which all who need it will be aided by their fellow human beings. A society of peace and prosperity for all. In short, a better world than the one we live in now. Is such a world even possible, or is it nothing more than wishful thinking? Is it a dream world, a utopia that can never become real?

There was a long period of time where man still lived like an animal among the animals, the Animalium. We all know that man outgrew animal life. After all, he discovered culture, a find that lifted man from the life of hunting and gathering that all animals need to continue their life on earth. Ever since man has been on a road towards a human, humane existence. That is the better world to which this book is dedicated. It is the time of the Humanium.

But it is true that one has not been able to reach the Humanium yet. He still resides in the transitional era, the Transitium.

In this time man has not completely rid himself of the primitive animalistic features. You will find a list of those in this book.

However, in our time a current has emerged that prepares us for when we reach the Humanium. These are the people who are caught by the concept of a humane society and who are already working reaching it. It is the historical task of the current man to help his contemporaries leave behind the primitive features of the Transitium. The Humanium is a better world that lies before us. Let all people of good will gather in a movement for a better world by ending the system of states and establish a world government.

I wish you the best of luck!